Electronic Discovery
Complete Self-Assessment Guide

The guidance in this Self-Assessment is based on Electronic Discovery best practices and standards in business process architecture, design and quality management. The guidance is also based on the professional judgment of the individual collaborators listed in the Acknowledgments.

Notice of rights

Trademarks

CW01497146

Table of Contents

About The Art of Service

The Art of Service, Business Process Architects since 2000, is dedicated to helping business achieve excellence.

Defining, designing, creating, and implementing a process to solve a business challenge or meet a business objective is the most valuable role... In EVERY company, organization and department.

Unless you're talking a one-time, single-use project within a business, there should be a process. Whether that process is managed and implemented by humans, AI, or a combination of the two, it needs to be designed by someone with a complex enough perspective to ask the right questions.

Someone capable of asking the right questions and step back and say, 'What are we really trying to accomplish here? And is there a different way to look at it?'

With The Art of Service's Business Process Architect Self-Assessments, Research, Toolkits, Education and Certifications we empower people who can do just that — whether their title is marketer, entrepreneur, manager, salesperson, consultant, Business Process Manager, executive assistant, IT Manager, CIO etc... —they are the people who rule the future. They are people who watch the process as it happens, and ask the right questions to make the process work better.

Contact us when you need any support with this Self-Assessment and any help with templates, blue-prints and examples of standard documents you might need:

http://theartofservice.com
service@theartofservice.com

Acknowledgments

This checklist was developed under the auspices of The Art of Service, chaired by Gerardus Blokdyk.

Representatives from several client companies participated in the preparation of this Self-Assessment.

Our deepest gratitude goes out to Matt Champagne, Ph.D. Surveys Expert, for his invaluable help and advise in structuring the Self Assessment.

Mr Champagne can be contacted at http://matthewchampagne.com/

In addition, we are thankful for the design and printing services provided.

Included Resources - how to access

Included with your purchase of the book is the Electronic Discovery Self-Assessment downloadable resource, which contains all questions and Self-Assessment areas of this book.

Get it now- you will be glad you did - do it now, before you forget.

How? Simply send an email to **access@theartofservice.com** with this books' title in the subject to get all the Electronic Discovery Self-Assessment questions in a ready to use Excel spreadsheet, containing the self-assessment, graphs, and project RACI planning - all with examples to get you started right away.

Your feedback is invaluable to us

If you recently bought this book, we would love to hear from you! You can do this by writing a review on amazon (or the online store where you purchased this book) about your last purchase! As part of our continual service improvement process, we love to hear real client experiences and feedback.

How does it work?
To post a review on Amazon, just log in to your account and click on the Create Your Own Review button (under Customer Reviews) of the relevant product page. You can find examples of product reviews in Amazon. If you purchased from another online store, simply follow their procedures.

What happens when I submit my review?
Once you have submitted your review, send us an email at review@theartofservice.com with the link to your review so we can properly thank you for your feedback.

Purpose of this Self-Assessment

This Self-Assessment has been developed to improve understanding of the requirements and elements of Electronic Discovery, based on best practices and standards in business process architecture, design and quality management.

It is designed to allow for a rapid Self-Assessment of an organization or facility to determine how closely existing management practices and procedures correspond to the elements of the Self-Assessment.

The criteria of requirements and elements of Electronic Discovery have been rephrased in the format of a Self-Assessment questionnaire, with a seven-criterion scoring system, as explained in this document.

In this format, even with limited background knowledge of

Electronic Discovery, a facility or other business manager can quickly review existing operations to determine how they measure up to the standards. This in turn can serve as the starting point of a 'gap analysis' to identify management tools or system elements that might usefully be implemented in the organization to help improve overall performance.

How to use the Self-Assessment

On the following pages are a series of questions to identify to what extent your Electronic Discovery initiative is complete in comparison to the requirements set in standards.

To facilitate answering the questions, there is a space in front of each question to enter a score on a scale of '1' to '5'.

1 Strongly Disagree

2 Disagree

3 Neutral

4 Agree

5 Strongly Agree

Read the question and rate it with the following in front of mind:

'In my belief,
the answer to this question is clearly defined'.

There are two ways in which you can choose to interpret this statement;

1. how aware are you that the answer to the question is clearly defined

2. for more in-depth analysis you can choose to gather evidence and confirm the answer to the question. This obviously will take more time, most Self-Assessment users opt for the first way to interpret the question and dig deeper later on based on the outcome of the overall Self-Assessment.

A score of '1' would mean that the answer is not clear at all, where a '5' would mean the answer is crystal clear and defined. Leave emtpy when the question is not applicable or you don't want to answer it, you can skip it without affecting your score. Write your score in the space provided.

After you have responded to all the appropriate statements in each section, compute your average score for that section, using the formula provided, and round to the nearest tenth. Then transfer to the corresponding spoke in the Electronic Discovery Scorecard on the second next page of the Self-Assessment.

Your completed Electronic Discovery Scorecard will give you a clear presentation of which Electronic Discovery areas need attention.

Electronic Discovery
Scorecard Example

Example of how the finalized Scorecard can look like:

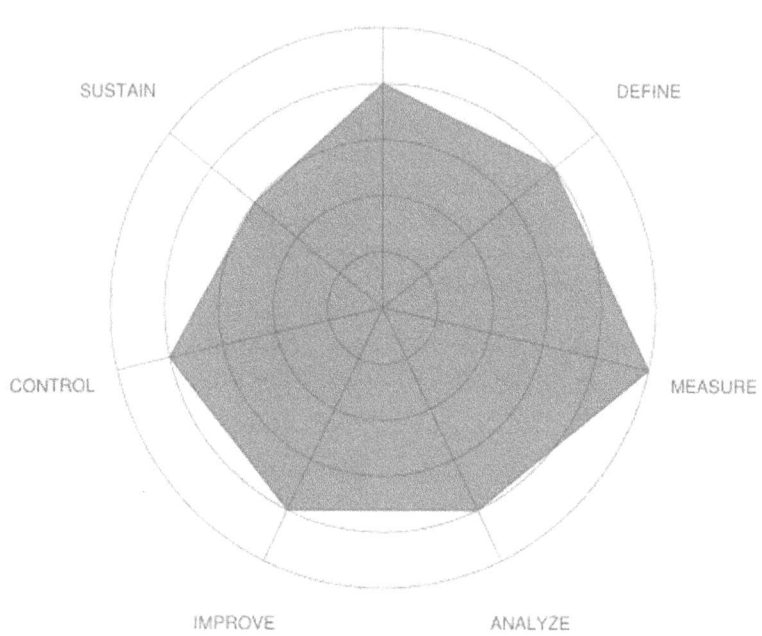

Electronic Discovery Scorecard

Your Scores:

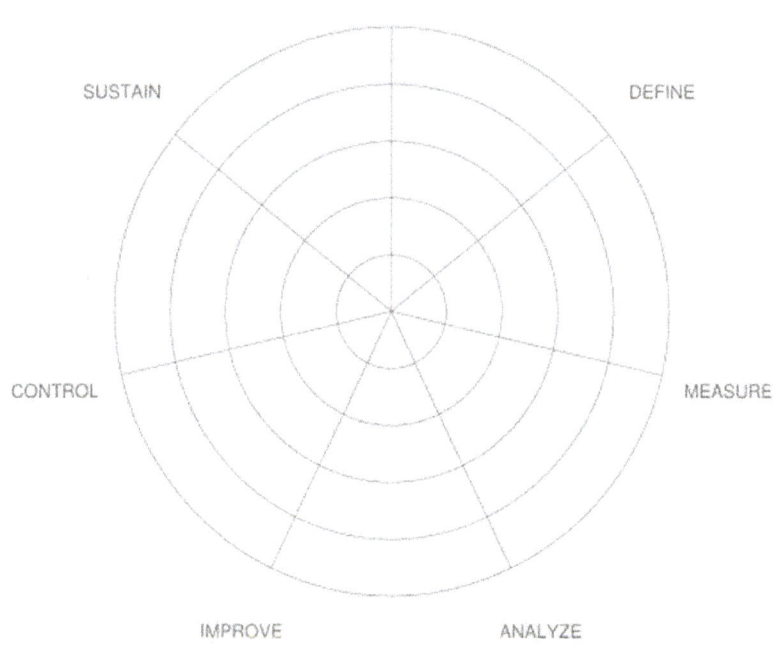

BEGINNING OF THE SELF-ASSESSMENT:

SELF-ASSESSMENT SECTION
START

CRITERION #1: RECOGNIZE

INTENT: Be aware of the need for change. Recognize that there is an unfavorable variation, problem or symptom.

In my belief, the answer to this question is clearly defined:

5 Strongly Agree

4 Agree

3 Neutral

2 Disagree

1 Strongly Disagree

1. What else needs to be measured?
<--- Score

2. **What tools and technologies are needed for a custom Electronic Discovery project?**
<--- Score

3. **What training and capacity building actions are needed to implement proposed reforms?**

<--- Score

4. What information do users need?
<--- Score

5. Are controls defined to recognize and contain problems?
<--- Score

6. What situation(s) led to this Electronic Discovery Self Assessment?
<--- Score

7. How much are sponsors, customers, partners, stakeholders involved in Electronic Discovery? In other words, what are the risks, if Electronic Discovery does not deliver successfully?
<--- Score

8. Can Management personnel recognize the monetary benefit of Electronic Discovery?
<--- Score

9. What does Electronic Discovery success mean to the stakeholders?
<--- Score

10. Think about the people you identified for your Electronic Discovery project and the project responsibilities you would assign to them. what kind of training do you think they would need to perform these responsibilities effectively?
<--- Score

11. For your Electronic Discovery project, identify and describe the business environment. is there

more than one layer to the business environment?
<--- Score

12. What vendors make products that address the Electronic Discovery needs?
<--- Score

13. What are the business objectives to be achieved with Electronic Discovery?
<--- Score

14. Will it solve real problems?
<--- Score

15. What do we need to start doing?
<--- Score

16. Does Electronic Discovery create potential expectations in other areas that need to be recognized and considered?
<--- Score

17. What would happen if Electronic Discovery weren't done?
<--- Score

18. Who defines the rules in relation to any given issue?
<--- Score

19. Are there Electronic Discovery problems defined?
<--- Score

20. Will Electronic Discovery deliverables need to be tested and, if so, by whom?
<--- Score

21. When a Electronic Discovery manager recognizes a problem, what options are available?
<--- Score

22. Who had the original idea?
<--- Score

23. How does it fit into our organizational needs and tasks?
<--- Score

24. How do we Identify specific Electronic Discovery investment and emerging trends?
<--- Score

25. What are the expected benefits of Electronic Discovery to the business?
<--- Score

26. What prevents me from making the changes I know will make me a more effective Electronic Discovery leader?
<--- Score

27. Will a response program recognize when a crisis occurs and provide some level of response?
<--- Score

28. What problems are you facing and how do you consider Electronic Discovery will circumvent those obstacles?
<--- Score

29. How are the Electronic Discovery's objectives aligned to the organization's overall business

strategy?
<--- Score

30. How can auditing be a preventative security measure?
<--- Score

31. Is it clear when you think of the day ahead of you what activities and tasks you need to complete?
<--- Score

32. What is the smallest subset of the problem we can usefully solve?
<--- Score

33. Why do we need to keep records?
<--- Score

34. Are there any specific expectations or concerns about the Electronic Discovery team, Electronic Discovery itself?
<--- Score

35. As a sponsor, customer or management, how important is it to meet goals, objectives?
<--- Score

36. Will new equipment/products be required to facilitate Electronic Discovery delivery for example is new software needed?
<--- Score

37. How are we going to measure success?
<--- Score

38. What prevents me from making the changes I know will make me a more effective leader?
<--- Score

39. Do we know what we need to know about this topic?
<--- Score

40. Are there recognized Electronic Discovery problems?
<--- Score

41. Who else hopes to benefit from it?
<--- Score

Add up total points for this section:
_____ = Total points for this section

Divided by: _____ (number of statements answered) = _____
Average score for this section

Transfer your score to the Electronic Discovery Index at the beginning of the Self-Assessment.

SELF-ASSESSMENT SECTION
START

CRITERION #2: DEFINE:

INTENT: Formulate the business problem. Define the problem, needs and objectives.

In my belief, the answer to this question is clearly defined:

5 Strongly Agree

4 Agree

3 Neutral

2 Disagree

1 Strongly Disagree

1. Is the improvement team aware of the different versions of a process: what they think it is vs. what it actually is vs. what it should be vs. what it could be?
<--- Score

2. Is the current 'as is' process being followed? If not, what are the discrepancies?
<--- Score

3. What defines Best in Class?

<--- Score

4. Have all basic functions of Electronic Discovery been defined?
<--- Score

5. Have specific policy objectives been defined?
<--- Score

6. Is the scope of Electronic Discovery defined?
<--- Score

7. Are improvement team members fully trained on Electronic Discovery?
<--- Score

8. Is there a completed, verified, and validated high-level 'as is' (not 'should be' or 'could be') business process map?
<--- Score

9. What are the compelling business reasons for embarking on Electronic Discovery?
<--- Score

10. Is Electronic Discovery currently on schedule according to the plan?
<--- Score

11. Are roles and responsibilities formally defined?
<--- Score

12. How can the value of Electronic Discovery be defined?
<--- Score

13. Is a fully trained team formed, supported, and committed to work on the Electronic Discovery improvements?
<--- Score

14. What are the rough order estimates on cost savings/opportunities that Electronic Discovery brings?
<--- Score

15. How and when will be baselines be defined?
<--- Score

16. Has a team charter been developed and communicated?
<--- Score

17. When was the Electronic Discovery start date?
<--- Score

18. Has everyone on the team, including the team leaders, been properly trained?
<--- Score

19. Are there different segments of customers?
<--- Score

20. Are business processes mapped?
<--- Score

21. How will the Electronic Discovery team and the organization measure complete success of Electronic Discovery?
<--- Score

22. Who are the Electronic Discovery improvement

team members, including Management Leads and Coaches?
<--- Score

23. Is data collected and displayed to better understand customer(s) critical needs and requirements.
<--- Score

24. When are meeting minutes sent out? Who is on the distribution list?
<--- Score

25. How would you define the culture here?
<--- Score

26. Is there a critical path to deliver Electronic Discovery results?
<--- Score

27. Are different versions of process maps needed to account for the different types of inputs?
<--- Score

28. How was the 'as is' process map developed, reviewed, verified and validated?
<--- Score

29. Has a high-level 'as is' process map been completed, verified and validated?
<--- Score

30. Are customers identified and high impact areas defined?
<--- Score

31. How do you keep key subject matter experts in the loop?
<--- Score

32. Is the team equipped with available and reliable resources?
<--- Score

33. Has the direction changed at all during the course of Electronic Discovery? If so, when did it change and why?
<--- Score

34. What are the Roles and Responsibilities for each team member and its leadership? Where is this documented?
<--- Score

35. Who defines (or who defined) the rules and roles?
<--- Score

36. Are there any constraints known that bear on the ability to perform Electronic Discovery work? How is the team addressing them?
<--- Score

37. Is there a completed SIPOC representation, describing the Suppliers, Inputs, Process, Outputs, and Customers?
<--- Score

38. What critical content must be communicated – who, what, when, where, and how?
<--- Score

39. Are Required Metrics Defined?

<--- Score

40. How did the Electronic Discovery manager receive input to the development of a Electronic Discovery improvement plan and the estimated completion dates/times of each activity?
<--- Score

41. Has the improvement team collected the 'voice of the customer' (obtained feedback – qualitative and quantitative)?
<--- Score

42. Do the requirements that we've gathered and the models that demonstrate them constitute a full and accurate representation of what we want?
<--- Score

43. Will team members regularly document their Electronic Discovery work?
<--- Score

44. If substitutes have been appointed, have they been briefed on the Electronic Discovery goals and received regular communications as to the progress to date?
<--- Score

45. In what way can we redefine the criteria of choice clients have in our category in our favor?
<--- Score

46. Have all of the relationships been defined properly?
<--- Score

47. What tools and roadmaps did you use for getting through the Define phase?
<--- Score

48. Has a project plan, Gantt chart, or similar been developed/completed?
<--- Score

49. Are audit criteria, scope, frequency and methods defined?
<--- Score

50. What sources do you use to gather information for a Electronic Discovery study?
<--- Score

51. Is the team sponsored by a champion or business leader?
<--- Score

52. Are approval levels defined for contracts and supplements to contracts?
<--- Score

53. What constraints exist that might impact the team?
<--- Score

54. Are security/privacy roles and responsibilities formally defined?
<--- Score

55. What key business process output measure(s) does Electronic Discovery leverage and how?
<--- Score

56. Is the team formed and are team leaders (Coaches and Management Leads) assigned?
<--- Score

57. Does the team have regular meetings?
<--- Score

58. How is the team tracking and documenting its work?
<--- Score

59. How and when will baselines be defined?
<--- Score

60. Is it clearly defined in and to your organization what you do?
<--- Score

61. When is the estimated completion date?
<--- Score

62. What would be the goal or target for a Electronic Discovery's improvement team?
<--- Score

63. Do we all define Electronic Discovery in the same way?
<--- Score

64. What specifically is the problem? Where does it occur? When does it occur? What is its extent?
<--- Score

65. Is there a Electronic Discovery management charter, including business case, problem and goal statements, scope, milestones, roles and

responsibilities, communication plan?
<--- Score

66. Has the Electronic Discovery work been fairly and/or equitably divided and delegated among team members who are qualified and capable to perform the work? Has everyone contributed?
<--- Score

67. Are task requirements clearly defined?
<--- Score

68. What are the boundaries of the scope? What is in bounds and what is not? What is the start point? What is the stop point?
<--- Score

69. Will team members perform Electronic Discovery work when assigned and in a timely fashion?
<--- Score

70. In what way can we redefine the criteria of choice in our category in our favor, as Method introduced style and design to cleaning and Virgin America returned glamor to flying?
<--- Score

71. Are accountability and ownership for Electronic Discovery clearly defined?
<--- Score

72. Is there regularly 100% attendance at the team meetings? If not, have appointed substitutes attended to preserve cross-functionality and full representation?
<--- Score

73. What are the dynamics of the communication plan?
<--- Score

74. What Organizational Structure is Required?
<--- Score

75. Is full participation by members in regularly held team meetings guaranteed?
<--- Score

76. Has/have the customer(s) been identified?
<--- Score

77. Are customer(s) identified and segmented according to their different needs and requirements?
<--- Score

78. Is the team adequately staffed with the desired cross-functionality? If not, what additional resources are available to the team?
<--- Score

79. How often are the team meetings?
<--- Score

80. Do the problem and goal statements meet the SMART criteria (specific, measurable, attainable, relevant, and time-bound)?
<--- Score

81. How will variation in the actual durations of each activity be dealt with to ensure that the expected Electronic Discovery results are met?
<--- Score

82. What customer feedback methods were used to solicit their input?
<--- Score

83. Is the Electronic Discovery scope manageable?
<--- Score

84. Is Electronic Discovery linked to key business goals and objectives?
<--- Score

85. Are team charters developed?
<--- Score

86. Have the customer needs been translated into specific, measurable requirements? How?
<--- Score

87. How does the Electronic Discovery manager ensure against scope creep?
<--- Score

88. What baselines are required to be defined and managed?
<--- Score

89. How would one define Electronic Discovery leadership?
<--- Score

90. Has anyone else (internal or external to the organization) attempted to solve this problem or a similar one before? If so, what knowledge can be leveraged from these previous efforts?
<--- Score

Add up total points for this section:
_____ = Total points for this section

Divided by: _____ (number of
statements answered) = _____
Average score for this section

Transfer your score to the Electronic
Discovery Index at the beginning of the
Self-Assessment.

SELF-ASSESSMENT SECTION
START

CRITERION #3: MEASURE:

INTENT: Gather the correct data. Measure the current performance and evolution of the situation.

In my belief, the answer to this question is clearly defined:

5 Strongly Agree

4 Agree

3 Neutral

2 Disagree

1 Strongly Disagree

1. How can we measure the performance?
<--- Score

2. What does the charts tell us in terms of variation?
<--- Score

3. How do you identify and analyze stakeholders and their interests?
<--- Score

4. What should be measured?
<--- Score

5. How can you measure Electronic Discovery in a systematic way?
<--- Score

6. What particular quality tools did the team find helpful in establishing measurements?
<--- Score

7. Are process variation components displayed/ communicated using suitable charts, graphs, plots?
<--- Score

8. How will effects be measured?
<--- Score

9. Meeting the Challenge: Are Missed Electronic Discovery opportunities Costing you Money?
<--- Score

10. What evidence is there and what is measured?
<--- Score

11. Have you found any 'ground fruit' or 'low-hanging fruit' for immediate remedies to the gap in performance?
<--- Score

12. Why do the measurements/indicators matter?
<--- Score

13. Meeting the challenge: are missed Electronic Discovery opportunities costing us money?
<--- Score

14. What is the right balance of time and resources between investigation, analysis, and discussion and dissemination?

<--- Score

15. Does Electronic Discovery analysis show the relationships among important Electronic Discovery factors?

<--- Score

16. How to measure lifecycle phases?

<--- Score

17. What about Electronic Discovery Analysis of results?

<--- Score

18. Are key measures identified and agreed upon?

<--- Score

19. What potential environmental factors impact the Electronic Discovery effort?

<--- Score

20. Are we taking our company in the direction of better and revenue or cheaper and cost?

<--- Score

21. How large is the gap between current performance and the customer-specified (goal) performance?

<--- Score

22. What has the team done to assure the stability and accuracy of the measurement process?

<--- Score

23. Have the types of risks that may impact Electronic Discovery been identified and analyzed?
<--- Score

24. Who should receive measurement reports ?
<--- Score

25. What are the costs of reform?
<--- Score

26. What are your key indicators that you will measure, analyze and track?
<--- Score

27. Why does this measure/indicator matter?
<--- Score

28. Is long term and short term variability accounted for?
<--- Score

29. Are high impact defects defined and identified in the business process?
<--- Score

30. Is data collection planned and executed?
<--- Score

31. How do you measure success?
<--- Score

32. Is data collected on key measures that were identified?
<--- Score

33. How is the value delivered by Electronic Discovery being measured?
<--- Score

34. How will you measure your Electronic Discovery effectiveness?
<--- Score

35. How to measure variability?
<--- Score

36. What measurements are being captured?
<--- Score

37. Is Process Variation Displayed/Communicated?
<--- Score

38. Do we effectively measure and reward individual and team performance?
<--- Score

39. What is an unallowable cost?
<--- Score

40. Have changes been properly/adequately analyzed for effect?
<--- Score

41. How Will We Measure Success?
<--- Score

42. Is the solution cost-effective?
<--- Score

43. How will measures be used to manage and adapt?

<--- Score

44. What data was collected (past, present, future/ongoing)?
<--- Score

45. What are the key input variables? What are the key process variables? What are the key output variables?
<--- Score

46. What to measure and why?
<--- Score

47. Will We Aggregate Measures across Priorities?
<--- Score

48. Are the measurements objective?
<--- Score

49. What are the uncertainties surrounding estimates of impact?
<--- Score

50. Where is it measured?
<--- Score

51. Among the Electronic Discovery product and service cost to be estimated, which is considered hardest to estimate?
<--- Score

52. What measurements are possible, practicable and meaningful?
<--- Score

53. Does the Electronic Discovery task fit the

client's priorities?

<--- Score

54. Is performance measured?

<--- Score

55. Have the concerns of stakeholders to help identify and define potential barriers been obtained and analyzed?

<--- Score

56. What are measures?

<--- Score

57. Which customers cant participate in our Electronic Discovery domain because they lack skills, wealth, or convenient access to existing solutions?

<--- Score

58. Why identify and analyze stakeholders and their interests?

<--- Score

59. Is key measure data collection planned and executed, process variation displayed and communicated and performance baselined?

<--- Score

60. What methods are feasible and acceptable to estimate the impact of reforms?

<--- Score

61. Does Electronic Discovery analysis isolate the fundamental causes of problems?

<--- Score

62. What are the agreed upon definitions of the high impact areas, defect(s), unit(s), and opportunities that will figure into the process capability metrics?
<--- Score

63. Are losses documented, analyzed, and remedial processes developed to prevent future losses?
<--- Score

64. Do staff have the necessary skills to collect, analyze, and report data?
<--- Score

65. Do we aggressively reward and promote the people who have the biggest impact on creating excellent Electronic Discovery services/products?
<--- Score

66. Why should we expend time and effort to implement measurement?
<--- Score

67. Customer Measures: How Do Customers See Us?
<--- Score

68. Which customers can't participate in our market because they lack skills, wealth, or convenient access to existing solutions?
<--- Score

69. What key measures identified indicate the performance of the business process?
<--- Score

70. What are my customers expectations and

measures?
<--- Score

71. How is progress measured?
<--- Score

72. What are the types and number of measures to use?
<--- Score

73. How do we do risk analysis of rare, cascading, catastrophic events?
<--- Score

74. What will be measured?
<--- Score

75. Does the practice systematically track and analyze outcomes related for accountability and quality improvement?
<--- Score

76. How will success or failure be measured?
<--- Score

77. Do we aggressively reward and promote the people who have the biggest impact on creating excellent products?
<--- Score

78. Is this an issue for analysis or intuition?
<--- Score

79. Are priorities and opportunities deployed to your suppliers, partners, and collaborators to ensure organizational alignment?

<--- Score

80. How frequently do you track measures?
<--- Score

81. Are the units of measure consistent?
<--- Score

82. How is Knowledge Management Measured?
<--- Score

83. When is Knowledge Management Measured?
<--- Score

84. Does Electronic Discovery systematically track
and analyze outcomes for accountability and quality
improvement?
<--- Score

85. Is there a Performance Baseline?
<--- Score

86. Why Measure?
<--- Score

87. Are you taking your company in the direction of
better and revenue or cheaper and cost?
<--- Score

88. Have all non-recommended alternatives been
analyzed in sufficient detail?
<--- Score

89. Which Stakeholder Characteristics Are Analyzed?
<--- Score

90. Are there any easy-to-implement alternatives to Electronic Discovery? Sometimes other solutions are available that do not require the cost implications of a full-blown project?
<--- Score

91. Was a data collection plan established?
<--- Score

92. What charts has the team used to display the components of variation in the process?
<--- Score

93. Is a solid data collection plan established that includes measurement systems analysis?
<--- Score

94. Is it possible to estimate the impact of unanticipated complexity such as wrong or failed assumptions, feedback, etc. on proposed reforms?
<--- Score

95. Who participated in the data collection for measurements?
<--- Score

96. How will your organization measure success?
<--- Score

97. What Relevant Entities could be measured?
<--- Score

98. Which methods and measures do you use to determine workforce engagement and workforce satisfaction?
<--- Score

99. Can We Measure the Return on Analysis?
<--- Score

100. Are there measurements based on task performance?
<--- Score

101. How are you going to measure success?
<--- Score

102. How are measurements made?
<--- Score

Add up total points for this section:
_ _ _ _ _ = Total points for this section

Divided by: _ _ _ _ _ _ (number of statements answered) = _ _ _ _ _ _
Average score for this section

Transfer your score to the Electronic Discovery Index at the beginning of the Self-Assessment.

SELF-ASSESSMENT SECTION
START

CRITERION #4: ANALYZE:

INTENT: Analyze causes, assumptions and hypotheses.

In my belief, the answer to this question is clearly defined:

5 Strongly Agree

4 Agree

3 Neutral

2 Disagree

1 Strongly Disagree

1. What are the revised rough estimates of the financial savings/opportunity for Electronic Discovery improvements?
<--- Score

2. What controls do we have in place to protect data?
<--- Score

3. Did any additional data need to be collected?
<--- Score

4. What were the financial benefits resulting from any 'ground fruit or low-hanging fruit' (quick fixes)?
<--- Score

5. What are your current levels and trends in key measures or indicators of Electronic Discovery product and process performance that are important to and directly serve your customers? how do these results compare with the performance of your competi tors and other organizations with similar offerings?
<--- Score

6. What did the team gain from developing a sub-process map?
<--- Score

7. What process should we select for improvement?
<--- Score

8. Have any additional benefits been identified that will result from closing all or most of the gaps?
<--- Score

9. Was a detailed process map created to amplify critical steps of the 'as is' business process?
<--- Score

10. Is the Electronic Discovery process severely broken such that a re-design is necessary?
<--- Score

11. How was the detailed process map generated, verified, and validated?
<--- Score

12. Is Data and process analysis, root cause analysis and quantifying the gap/opportunity in place?
<--- Score

13. What are the disruptive Electronic Discovery technologies that enable our organization to radically change our business processes?
<--- Score

14. What conclusions were drawn from the team's data collection and analysis? How did the team reach these conclusions?
<--- Score

15. What does the data say about the performance of the business process?
<--- Score

16. How often will data be collected for measures?
<--- Score

17. What quality tools were used to get through the analyze phase?
<--- Score

18. Record-keeping requirements flow from the records needed as inputs, outputs, controls and for transformation of a Electronic Discovery process. ask yourself: are the records needed as inputs to the Electronic Discovery process available?
<--- Score

19. What successful thing are we doing today that may be blinding us to new growth opportunities?
<--- Score

20. What tools were used to narrow the list of possible causes?
<--- Score

21. How do mission and objectives affect the Electronic Discovery processes of our organization?
<--- Score

22. Do our leaders quickly bounce back from setbacks?
<--- Score

23. Was a cause-and-effect diagram used to explore the different types of causes (or sources of variation)?
<--- Score

24. What project management qualifications does the Project Manager have?
<--- Score

25. An organizationally feasible system request is one that considers the mission, goals and objectives of the organization. key questions are: is the solution request practical and will it solve a problem or take advantage of an opportunity to achieve company goals?
<--- Score

26. Identify an operational issue in your organization. for example, could a particular task be done more quickly or more efficiently?
<--- Score

27. What other organizational variables, such as reward systems or communication systems, affect

the performance of this Electronic Discovery process?
<--- Score

28. Have the problem and goal statements been updated to reflect the additional knowledge gained from the analyze phase?
<--- Score

29. What other jobs or tasks affect the performance of the steps in the Electronic Discovery process?
<--- Score

30. Were Pareto charts (or similar) used to portray the 'heavy hitters' (or key sources of variation)?
<--- Score

31. Were any designed experiments used to generate additional insight into the data analysis?
<--- Score

32. Is the performance gap determined?
<--- Score

33. What is the cost of poor quality as supported by the team's analysis?
<--- Score

34. When conducting a business process reengineering study, what should we look for when trying to identify business processes to change?
<--- Score

35. How do we promote understanding that

opportunity for improvement is not criticism of the status quo, or the people who created the status quo?

<--- Score

36. Is the suppliers process defined and controlled?

<--- Score

37. What are the best opportunities for value improvement?

<--- Score

38. How is the way you as the leader think and process information affecting your organizational culture?

<--- Score

39. Do you, as a leader, bounce back quickly from setbacks?

<--- Score

40. Were there any improvement opportunities identified from the process analysis?

<--- Score

41. What were the crucial 'moments of truth' on the process map?

<--- Score

42. Is the gap/opportunity displayed and communicated in financial terms?

<--- Score

43. How does the organization define, manage, and improve its Electronic Discovery processes?

<--- Score

44. Do your employees have the opportunity to do what they do best everyday?
<--- Score

45. What tools were used to generate the list of possible causes?
<--- Score

46. What kind of crime could a potential new hire have committed that would not only not disqualify him/her from being hired by our organization, but would actually indicate that he/she might be a particularly good fit?
<--- Score

47. Did any value-added analysis or 'lean thinking' take place to identify some of the gaps shown on the 'as is' process map?
<--- Score

48. Think about some of the processes you undertake within your organization. which do you own?
<--- Score

49. Are gaps between current performance and the goal performance identified?
<--- Score

50. How do you measure the Operational performance of your key work systems and processes, including productivity, cycle time, and other appropriate measures of process effectiveness, efficiency, and innovation?
<--- Score

51. Where is the data coming from to measure compliance?
<--- Score

Add up total points for this section:
_____ = Total points for this section

Divided by: _____ (number of
statements answered) = _____
Average score for this section

Transfer your score to the Electronic
Discovery Index at the beginning of the
Self-Assessment.

SELF-ASSESSMENT SECTION START

CRITERION #5: IMPROVE:

INTENT: Develop a practical solution. Innovate, establish and test the solution and to measure the results.

In my belief, the answer to this question is clearly defined:

5 Strongly Agree

4 Agree

3 Neutral

2 Disagree

1 Strongly Disagree

1. What actually has to improve and by how much?
<--- Score

2. How do we go about Comparing Electronic Discovery approaches/solutions?
<--- Score

3. How do we measure risk?
<--- Score

4. Who controls key decisions that will be made?
<--- Score

5. What is the implementation plan?
<--- Score

6. What evaluation strategy is needed and what needs to be done to assure its implementation and use?
<--- Score

7. Was a pilot designed for the proposed solution(s)?
<--- Score

8. Are possible solutions generated and tested?
<--- Score

9. Were any criteria developed to assist the team in testing and evaluating potential solutions?
<--- Score

10. What tools were most useful during the improve phase?
<--- Score

11. In the past few months, what is the smallest change we have made that has had the biggest positive result? What was it about that small change that produced the large return?
<--- Score

12. How do we improve productivity?
<--- Score

13. What is the team's contingency plan for potential problems occurring in implementation?

<--- Score

14. How will you know that you have improved?
<--- Score

15. Is a solution implementation plan established, including schedule/work breakdown structure, resources, risk management plan, cost/budget, and control plan?
<--- Score

16. Is the implementation plan designed?
<--- Score

17. What attendant changes will need to be made to ensure that the solution is successful?
<--- Score

18. What were the underlying assumptions on the cost-benefit analysis?
<--- Score

19. Risk factors: what are the characteristics of Electronic Discovery that make it risky?
<--- Score

20. Is pilot data collected and analyzed?
<--- Score

21. How will we know that a change is improvement?
<--- Score

22. What does the 'should be' process map/design look like?
<--- Score

23. How does the solution remove the key sources of issues discovered in the analyze phase?
<--- Score

24. What tools were used to tap into the creativity and encourage 'outside the box' thinking?
<--- Score

25. How Do We Link Measurement and Risk?
<--- Score

26. How did the team generate the list of possible solutions?
<--- Score

27. How can we improve performance?
<--- Score

28. What is Electronic Discovery's impact on utilizing the best solution(s)?
<--- Score

29. Are the best solutions selected?
<--- Score

30. How will the team or the process owner(s) monitor the implementation plan to see that it is working as intended?
<--- Score

31. Who are the people involved in developing and implementing Electronic Discovery?
<--- Score

32. Are we Assessing Electronic Discovery and Risk?
<--- Score

33. What tools do you use once you have decided on a Electronic Discovery strategy and more importantly how do you choose?
<--- Score

34. What do we want to improve?
<--- Score

35. To what extent does management recognize Electronic Discovery as a tool to increase the results?
<--- Score

36. Who controls the risk?
<--- Score

37. How do you use other indicators, such as workforce retention, absenteeism, grievances, safety, and productivity, to assess and improve workforce engagement?
<--- Score

38. How does the team improve its work?
<--- Score

39. What communications are necessary to support the implementation of the solution?
<--- Score

40. Who will be responsible for documenting the Electronic Discovery requirements in detail?
<--- Score

41. Is a contingency plan established?
<--- Score

42. What to do with the results or outcomes of measurements?
<--- Score

43. Who will be using the results of the measurement activities?
<--- Score

44. If you could go back in time five years, what decision would you make differently? what is your best guess as to what decision youre making today you might regret five years from now?
<--- Score

45. Is the optimal solution selected based on testing and analysis?
<--- Score

46. What error proofing will be done to address some of the discrepancies observed in the 'as is' process?
<--- Score

47. Describe the design of the pilot and what tests were conducted, if any?
<--- Score

48. What needs improvement?
<--- Score

49. Does the goal represent a desired result that can be measured?
<--- Score

50. How to Improve?
<--- Score

51. How do you improve your likelihood of success ?
<--- Score

52. What resources are required for the improvement effort?
<--- Score

53. How do we measure improved Electronic Discovery service perception, and satisfaction?
<--- Score

54. What improvements have been achieved?
<--- Score

55. In the past few months, what is the smallest change we have made that has had the biggest positive result? what was it about that small change that produced the large return?
<--- Score

56. Is there a cost/benefit analysis of optimal solution(s)?
<--- Score

57. How do you measure progress and evaluate training effectiveness?
<--- Score

58. How can skill-level changes improve Electronic Discovery?
<--- Score

59. Is there a small-scale pilot for proposed improvement(s)? What conclusions were drawn from the outcomes of a pilot?
<--- Score

60. What is the magnitude of the improvements?
<--- Score

61. At what point will vulnerability assessments be performed once Electronic Discovery is put into production (e.g., ongoing Risk Management after implementation)?
<--- Score

62. How do you improve workforce health, safety, and security? what are your performance measures and improvement goals for each of these workforce needs? what are any significant differences in these factors and performance measures or targets for different workplace environments?
<--- Score

63. How can we improve Electronic Discovery?
<--- Score

64. What lessons, if any, from a pilot were incorporated into the design of the full-scale solution?
<--- Score

65. Who will be responsible for making the decisions to include or exclude requested changes once Electronic Discovery is underway?
<--- Score

66. What can we do to improve?
<--- Score

67. Why improve in the first place?
<--- Score

68. How significant is the improvement in the eyes of the end user?
<--- Score

69. How do we keep improving Electronic Discovery?
<--- Score

70. How do we Improve Electronic Discovery service perception, and satisfaction?
<--- Score

71. How will you know when its improved?
<--- Score

72. What are the implications of this decision 10 minutes, 10 months, and 10 years from now?
<--- Score

73. Is there a high likelihood that any recommendations will achieve their intended results?
<--- Score

74. Is the measure understandable to a variety of people?
<--- Score

75. Can the solution be designed and implemented within an acceptable time period?
<--- Score

76. Are there any constraints (technical, political, cultural, or otherwise) that would inhibit certain solutions?
<--- Score

77. How will you measure the results?
<--- Score

78. Is the solution technically practical?
<--- Score

79. How will the organization know that the solution worked?
<--- Score

80. Are improved process ('should be') maps modified based on pilot data and analysis?
<--- Score

81. What went well, what should change, what can improve?
<--- Score

82. If you could go back in time five years, what decision would you make differently? What is your best guess as to what decision you're making today you might regret five years from now?
<--- Score

83. What tools were used to evaluate the potential solutions?
<--- Score

84. Are new and improved process ('should be') maps developed?
<--- Score

85. How do we decide how much to remunerate an employee?
<--- Score

86. Risk events: what are the things that could go wrong?

<--- Score

Add up total points for this section:

_ _ _ _ _ = Total points for this section

Divided by: _ _ _ _ _ _ (number of statements answered) = _ _ _ _ _ _
Average score for this section

Transfer your score to the Electronic Discovery Index at the beginning of the Self-Assessment.

SELF-ASSESSMENT SECTION
START

CRITERION #6: CONTROL:

INTENT: Implement the practical
solution. Maintain the performance and
correct possible complications.

In my belief, the answer to this
question is clearly defined:

5 Strongly Agree

4 Agree

3 Neutral

2 Disagree

1 Strongly Disagree

1. What is our theory of human motivation, and how does our compensation plan fit with that view?
<--- Score

2. Whats the best design framework for Electronic Discovery organization now that, in a post industrial-age if the top-down, command and control model is no longer relevant?
<--- Score

3. Why is change control necessary?
<--- Score

4. Are documented procedures clear and easy to follow for the operators?
<--- Score

5. How will the process owner and team be able to hold the gains?
<--- Score

6. Do the decisions we make today help people and the planet tomorrow?
<--- Score

7. Is there a control plan in place for sustaining improvements (short and long-term)?
<--- Score

8. Are pertinent alerts monitored, analyzed and distributed to appropriate personnel?
<--- Score

9. If there currently is no plan, will a plan be developed?
<--- Score

10. Is there a recommended audit plan for routine surveillance inspections of Electronic Discovery's gains?
<--- Score

11. What do we stand for--and what are we against?
<--- Score

12. Are new process steps, standards, and documentation ingrained into normal operations?
<--- Score

13. What is your quality control system?
<--- Score

14. Is reporting being used or needed?
<--- Score

15. Are controls in place and consistently applied?
<--- Score

16. What should we measure to verify efficiency gains?
<--- Score

17. What other systems, operations, processes, and infrastructures (hiring practices, staffing, training, incentives/rewards, metrics/dashboards/scorecards, etc.) need updates, additions, changes, or deletions in order to facilitate knowledge transfer and improvements?
<--- Score

18. Is a response plan established and deployed?
<--- Score

19. Is there a transfer of ownership and knowledge to process owner and process team tasked with the responsibilities.
<--- Score

20. Does job training on the documented procedures need to be part of the process team's education and training?

<--- Score

21. What's the best design framework for an organization in a post Industrial-Age if the top-down, command and control model is no longer relevant?
<--- Score

22. Are suggested corrective/restorative actions indicated on the response plan for known causes to problems that might surface?
<--- Score

23. What are the known security controls?
<--- Score

24. What can you control?
<--- Score

25. How will input, process, and output variables be checked to detect for sub-optimal conditions?
<--- Score

26. Will existing staff require re-training, for example, to learn new business processes?
<--- Score

27. Who will be in control?
<--- Score

28. In the case of a Electronic Discovery project, the criteria for the audit derive from implementation objectives. an audit of a Electronic Discovery project involves assessing whether the recommendations outlined for implementation have been met. in other words, can we track that any Electronic Discovery project

is implemented as planned, and is it working?
<--- Score

29. Is knowledge gained on process shared and institutionalized?
<--- Score

30. How will the process owner verify improvement in present and future sigma levels, process capabilities?
<--- Score

31. What other areas of the organization might benefit from the Electronic Discovery team's improvements, knowledge, and learning?
<--- Score

32. How will new or emerging customer needs/requirements be checked/communicated to orient the process toward meeting the new specifications and continually reducing variation?
<--- Score

33. Is new knowledge gained imbedded in the response plan?
<--- Score

34. What is the recommended frequency of auditing?
<--- Score

35. What is your theory of human motivation, and how does your compensation plan fit with that view?
<--- Score

36. How do you encourage people to take control and responsibility?
<--- Score

37. What key inputs and outputs are being measured on an ongoing basis?
<--- Score

38. Are there documented procedures?
<--- Score

39. What should we measure to verify effectiveness gains?
<--- Score

40. Where do ideas that reach policy makers and planners as proposals for Electronic Discovery strengthening and reform actually originate?
<--- Score

41. Are operating procedures consistent?
<--- Score

42. Is there documentation that will support the successful operation of the improvement?
<--- Score

43. Does the response plan contain a definite closed loop continual improvement scheme (e.g., plan-do-check-act)?
<--- Score

44. Is there a documented and implemented monitoring plan?
<--- Score

45. Who is the Electronic Discovery process owner?
<--- Score

46. Against what alternative is success being measured?
<--- Score

47. How can we best use all of our knowledge repositories to enhance learning and sharing?
<--- Score

48. Is a response plan in place for when the input, process, or output measures indicate an 'out-of-control' condition?
<--- Score

49. Who has control over resources?
<--- Score

50. How do you encourage people to take control and responsibility?
<--- Score

51. What are we attempting to measure/monitor?
<--- Score

52. What is the control/monitoring plan?
<--- Score

53. Does the Electronic Discovery performance meet the customer's requirements?
<--- Score

54. What are the key elements of your Electronic Discovery performance improvement system, including your evaluation, organizational learning, and innovation processes?
<--- Score

55. Do the Electronic Discovery decisions we make today help people and the planet tomorrow?
<--- Score

56. Do you monitor the effectiveness of your Electronic Discovery activities?
<--- Score

57. How do controls support value?
<--- Score

58. Were the planned controls in place?
<--- Score

59. Is there a standardized process?
<--- Score

60. What are the critical parameters to watch?
<--- Score

61. What quality tools were useful in the control phase?
<--- Score

62. How will report readings be checked to effectively monitor performance?
<--- Score

63. Who controls critical resources?
<--- Score

64. Does a troubleshooting guide exist or is it needed?
<--- Score

65. What should the next improvement project be that is related to Electronic Discovery?

<--- Score

66. What are we attempting to measure/monitor?
<--- Score

67. Have new or revised work instructions resulted?
<--- Score

68. What are your results for key measures or indicators of the accomplishment of your Electronic Discovery strategy and action plans, including building and strengthening core competencies?
<--- Score

69. What do we stand for--and what are we against?
<--- Score

70. Will any special training be provided for results interpretation?
<--- Score

71. Does Electronic Discovery appropriately measure and monitor risk?
<--- Score

72. How will the day-to-day responsibilities for monitoring and continual improvement be transferred from the improvement team to the process owner?
<--- Score

73. Has the improved process and its steps been standardized?
<--- Score

74. How might the organization capture best practices and lessons learned so as to leverage improvements across the business?
<--- Score

75. Were the planned controls working?
<--- Score

76. How do our controls stack up?
<--- Score

Add up total points for this section:
_ _ _ _ _ = Total points for this section

Divided by: _ _ _ _ _ _ (number of statements answered) = _ _ _ _ _ _
Average score for this section

Transfer your score to the Electronic Discovery Index at the beginning of the Self-Assessment.

SELF-ASSESSMENT SECTION START

CRITERION #7: SUSTAIN:

INTENT: Retain the benefits.

In my belief, the answer to this question is clearly defined:

5 Strongly Agree

4 Agree

3 Neutral

2 Disagree

1 Strongly Disagree

1. Which individuals, teams or departments will be involved in Electronic Discovery?
<--- Score

2. Are we / should we be Revolutionary or evolutionary?
<--- Score

3. Who do we want out customers to become?
<--- Score

4. What is your BATNA (best alternative to a negotiated agreement)?

<--- Score

5. You may have created your customer policies at a time when you lacked resources, technology wasn't up-to-snuff, or low service levels were the industry norm. Have those circumstances changed?
<--- Score

6. Will there be any necessary staff changes (redundancies or new hires)?
<--- Score

7. How will you motivate the dishwashers?
<--- Score

8. Has the investment re-baselined during the past fiscal year?
<--- Score

9. If you had to rebuild your organization without any traditional competitive advantages (i.e., no killer a technology, promising research, innovative product/service delivery model, etc.), how would your people have to approach their work and collaborate together in order to create the necessary conditions for success?
<--- Score

10. How can you negotiate Electronic Discovery successfully with a stubborn boss, an irate client, or a deceitful coworker?
<--- Score

11. What did we miss in the interview for the worst hire we ever made?

<--- Score

12. Do you see more potential in people than they do in themselves?
<--- Score

13. Who will determine interim and final deadlines?
<--- Score

14. Who are four people whose careers I've enhanced?
<--- Score

15. What are the rules and assumptions my industry operates under? What if the opposite were true?
<--- Score

16. What potential megatrends could make our business model obsolete?
<--- Score

17. How do we maintain Electronic Discovery's Integrity?
<--- Score

18. How do we focus on what is right -not who is right?
<--- Score

19. What stupid rule would we most like to kill?
<--- Score

20. How do we provide a safe environment -physically and emotionally?
<--- Score

21. How does Electronic Discovery integrate with

other business initiatives?
<--- Score

22. Why is it important to have senior management support for a Electronic Discovery project?
<--- Score

23. If our customer were my grandmother, would I tell her to buy what we're selling?
<--- Score

24. What counts that we are not counting?
<--- Score

25. How is business? Why?
<--- Score

26. What is something you believe that nearly no one agrees with you on?
<--- Score

27. In a project to restructure Electronic Discovery outcomes, which stakeholders would you involve?
<--- Score

28. How do we Lead with Electronic Discovery in Mind?
<--- Score

29. Do you have an implicit bias for capital investments over people investments?
<--- Score

30. How do we foster the skills, knowledge, talents, attributes, and characteristics we want to

have?
<--- Score

31. What business benefits will Electronic Discovery goals deliver if achieved?
<--- Score

32. What will be the consequences to the business (financial, reputation etc) if Electronic Discovery does not go ahead or fails to deliver the objectives?
<--- Score

33. If no one would ever find out about my accomplishments, how would I lead differently?
<--- Score

34. What External Factors Influence Our Success?
<--- Score

35. What are strategies for increasing support and reducing opposition?
<--- Score

36. What am I trying to prove to myself, and how might it be hijacking my life and business success?
<--- Score

37. How likely is it that a customer would recommend our company to a friend or colleague?
<--- Score

38. What are we challenging, in the sense that Mac challenged the PC or Dove tackled the Beauty Myth?
<--- Score

39. Are assumptions made in Electronic Discovery

stated explicitly?
<--- Score

40. What one word do we want to own in the minds of our customers, employees, and partners?
<--- Score

41. Are the criteria for selecting recommendations stated?
<--- Score

42. Who sets the Electronic Discovery standards?
<--- Score

43. What happens at this company when people fail?
<--- Score

44. What is our Electronic Discovery Strategy?
<--- Score

45. Do I know what I'm doing? And who do I call if I don't?
<--- Score

46. Who are you going to put out of business, and why?
<--- Score

47. In what ways are Electronic Discovery vendors and us interacting to ensure safe and effective use?
<--- Score

48. Are there any disadvantages to implementing Electronic Discovery? There might be some that are less obvious?

<--- Score

49. How do we foster innovation?
<--- Score

50. What does your signature ensure?
<--- Score

51. How do we ensure that implementations of Electronic Discovery products are done in a way that ensures safety?
<--- Score

52. Think about the kind of project structure that would be appropriate for your Electronic Discovery project. should it be formal and complex, are can it be less formal and relatively simple?
<--- Score

53. What is Effective Electronic Discovery?
<--- Score

54. Do we have bad profits?
<--- Score

55. What should we stop doing?
<--- Score

56. Who is responsible for errors?
<--- Score

57. What is an unauthorized commitment?
<--- Score

58. Who is the main stakeholder, with ultimate

responsibility for driving Electronic Discovery forward?
<--- Score

59. Do they use it?
<--- Score

60. What are the success criteria that will indicate that Electronic Discovery objectives have been met and the benefits delivered?
<--- Score

61. Who will manage the integration of tools?
<--- Score

62. If we weren't already in this business, would we enter it today? And if not, what are we going to do about it?
<--- Score

63. If we got kicked out and the board brought in a new CEO, what would he do?
<--- Score

64. Has implementation been effective in reaching specified objectives?
<--- Score

65. How do we go about Securing Electronic Discovery?
<--- Score

66. What information is critical to our organization that our executives are ignoring?
<--- Score

67. Is the impact that Electronic Discovery has shown?
<--- Score

68. How would our PR, marketing, and social media change if we did not use outside agencies?
<--- Score

69. If you were responsible for initiating and implementing major changes in your organization, what steps might you take to ensure acceptance of those changes?
<--- Score

70. What role does communication play in the success or failure of a Electronic Discovery project?
<--- Score

71. Why are Electronic Discovery skills important?
<--- Score

72. Did my employees make progress today?
<--- Score

73. Have benefits been optimized with all key stakeholders?
<--- Score

74. Whom among your colleagues do you trust, and for what?
<--- Score

75. Is there any reason to believe the opposite of my current belief?
<--- Score

76. If energy were free, what would we do differently?

<--- Score

77. Political -is anyone trying to undermine this project?
<--- Score

78. Why don't our customers like us?
<--- Score

79. What trophy do we want on our mantle?
<--- Score

80. Do we have enough freaky customers in our portfolio pushing us to the limit day in and day out?
<--- Score

81. Which models, tools and techniques are necessary?
<--- Score

82. Am I failing differently each time?
<--- Score

83. If I had to leave my organization for a year and the only communication I could have with employees was a single paragraph, what would I write?
<--- Score

84. What management system can we use to leverage the Electronic Discovery experience, ideas, and concerns of the people closest to the work to be done?
<--- Score

85. How to deal with Electronic Discovery Changes?
<--- Score

86. Will it be accepted by users?
<--- Score

87. When information truly is ubiquitous, when reach and connectivity are completely global, when computing resources are infinite, and when a whole new set of impossibilities are not only possible, but happening, what will that do to our business?
<--- Score

88. Are there Electronic Discovery Models?
<--- Score

89. Is our strategy driving our strategy? Or is the way in which we allocate resources driving our strategy?
<--- Score

90. What is a feasible sequencing of reform initiatives over time?
<--- Score

91. To whom do you add value?
<--- Score

92. What is our question?
<--- Score

93. How are conflicts dealt with?
<--- Score

94. Whose voice (department, ethnic group, women, older workers, etc) might you have missed hearing from in your company, and how might you amplify this voice to create positive momentum for your business?

<--- Score

95. Who will provide the final approval of Electronic Discovery deliverables?
<--- Score

96. What is our Big Hairy Audacious Goal?
<--- Score

97. What may be the consequences for the performance of an organization if all stakeholders are not consulted regarding Electronic Discovery?
<--- Score

98. How can we become the company that would put us out of business?
<--- Score

99. Who, on the executive team or the board, has spoken to a customer recently?
<--- Score

100. Do we say no to customers for no reason?
<--- Score

101. Is Electronic Discovery dependent on the successful delivery of a current project?
<--- Score

102. How will we build a 100-year startup?
<--- Score

103. What are specific Electronic Discovery Rules to follow?
<--- Score

104. Legal and contractual - are we allowed to do this?
<--- Score

105. What is it like to work for me?
<--- Score

106. How much contingency will be available in the budget?
<--- Score

107. What are your most important goals for the strategic Electronic Discovery objectives?
<--- Score

108. What are the business goals Electronic Discovery is aiming to achieve?
<--- Score

109. What do we do when new problems arise?
<--- Score

110. Are we making progress? and are we making progress as Electronic Discovery leaders?
<--- Score

111. Instead of going to current contacts for new ideas, what if you reconnected with dormant contacts--the people you used to know? If you were going reactivate a dormant tie, who would it be?
<--- Score

112. Do we have the right capabilities and capacities?
<--- Score

113. Do we have the right people on the bus?
<--- Score

114. How do you govern and fulfill your societal responsibilities?
<--- Score

115. Economic -do we have the time and money?
<--- Score

116. What current systems have to be understood and/or changed?
<--- Score

117. Are we relevant? Will we be relevant five years from now? Ten?
<--- Score

118. Who have we, as a company, historically been when we've been at our best?
<--- Score

119. What are the top 3 things at the forefront of our Electronic Discovery agendas for the next 3 years?
<--- Score

120. Who will be responsible for deciding whether Electronic Discovery goes ahead or not after the initial investigations?
<--- Score

121. Who uses our product in ways we never expected?
<--- Score

122. In the past year, what have you done (or could you have done) to increase the accurate perception of this company/brand as ethical and honest?
<--- Score

123. What happens if you do not have enough funding?
<--- Score

124. Who is responsible for ensuring appropriate resources (time, people and money) are allocated to Electronic Discovery?
<--- Score

125. Would you rather sell to knowledgeable and informed customers or to uninformed customers?
<--- Score

126. In retrospect, of the projects that we pulled the plug on, what percent do we wish had been allowed to keep going, and what percent do we wish had ended earlier?
<--- Score

127. Are we changing as fast as the world around us?
<--- Score

128. Do you keep 50% of your time unscheduled?
<--- Score

129. Can we maintain our growth without detracting from the factors that have contributed to our success?
<--- Score

130. Who do we think the world wants us to be?

<--- Score

131. Where can we break convention?
<--- Score

132. Is maximizing Electronic Discovery protection the same as minimizing Electronic Discovery loss?
<--- Score

133. Operational - will it work?
<--- Score

134. How can we become more high-tech but still be high touch?
<--- Score

135. Who will determine interim and final deadlines?
<--- Score

136. How do you determine the key elements that affect Electronic Discovery workforce satisfaction? how are these elements determined for different workforce groups and segments?
<--- Score

137. Which functions and people interact with the supplier and or customer?
<--- Score

138. Were lessons learned captured and communicated?
<--- Score

139. What would have to be true for the option on the table to be the best possible choice?

<--- Score

140. Are we paying enough attention to the partners our company depends on to succeed?
<--- Score

141. How do we engage the workforce, in addition to satisfying them?
<--- Score

142. How do I stay inspired?
<--- Score

143. Are you satisfied with your current role? If not, what is missing from it?
<--- Score

144. How are we doing compared to our industry?
<--- Score

145. What is the range of capabilities?
<--- Score

146. Why should people listen to you?
<--- Score

147. How will you know that the Electronic Discovery project has been successful?
<--- Score

148. Do we think we know, or do we know we know ?
<--- Score

149. If our company went out of business tomorrow, would anyone who doesn't get a paycheck here care?

<--- Score

150. Ask yourself: how would we do this work if we only had one staff member to do it?
<--- Score

151. We picked a method, now what?
<--- Score

152. What will drive Electronic Discovery change?
<--- Score

153. What knowledge, skills and characteristics mark a good Electronic Discovery project manager?
<--- Score

154. What would I recommend my friend do if he were facing this dilemma?
<--- Score

155. Who are the key stakeholders?
<--- Score

156. Among our stronger employees, how many see themselves at the company in three years? How many would leave for a 10 percent raise from another company?
<--- Score

157. Schedule -can it be done in the given time?
<--- Score

158. What are your key business, operational, societal responsibility, and human resource strategic challenges and advantages?

<--- Score

159. Are new benefits received and understood?
<--- Score

160. What was the last experiment we ran?
<--- Score

161. Have new benefits been realized?
<--- Score

162. Do we underestimate the customer's journey?
<--- Score

163. What have we done to protect our business from competitive encroachment?
<--- Score

164. If you had to rebuild your organization without any traditional competitive advantages how would your people have to approach their work and collaborate together in order to create the necessary conditions for success?
<--- Score

165. What are the critical success factors?
<--- Score

166. Do I make eye contact 100 percent of the time?
<--- Score

167. How can we incorporate support to ensure safe and effective use of Electronic Discovery into the services that we provide?
<--- Score

168. Who else should we help?
<--- Score

169. What happens when a new employee joins the organization?
<--- Score

170. How to Secure Electronic Discovery?
<--- Score

171. What are the gaps in my knowledge and experience?
<--- Score

Add up total points for this section:
_____ = Total points for this section

Divided by: _____ (number of statements answered) = _____
Average score for this section

Transfer your score to the Electronic Discovery Index at the beginning of the Self-Assessment.

Index

Lightning Source UK Ltd.
Milton Keynes UK
UKHW021811220419
341415UK00009B/2408/P